Pizza

D1308238

by **Dana Meachen Rau**

Reading Consultant: Nanci R. Vargus, Ed.D.

Marshall Cavendish
Benchmark
New York

Picture Words

 cheese

 mushrooms

 onions

 peppers

 pizza

 tomatoes

3

A can be round.

A can be square.

A has crust and everywhere!

A can have .

A can have spots.

A can have .

A can be hot!

A can have
and , too.

A slice of for me.

A slice of for you.

Words to Know

crust (krust)
   the bread part of a pizza

mushroom (MUSH-room)
   a type of plant that grows in dirt

onion (UN-yuhn)
   a vegetable with a strong taste
   and smell

pepper (PEP-ehr)
   a sweet or hot vegetable with
   many seeds

Find Out More

Books

DK Publishing. *My Food Pyramid*. New York: DK Children, 2007.

Dobson, Christina. *Pizza Counting*. Watertown, MA: Charlesbridge Publishing, 2003.

Wagner, Lisa. *Cool Pizza to Make and Bake: Easy Recipes for Kids to Cook*. Edina, MN: Abdo Publishing, 2007.

Web Sites

Kids Health Recipes: Tiny Pizzas
www.kidshealth.org/kid/recipes/recipes/pizzas.html

Meals Matter: My Very Own Pizza
www.mealsmatter.org/CookingForFamily/Activities/pizza.aspx

PBS Kids: Cafe Zoom: Dessert Pizza
pbskids.org/zoom/activities/cafe/dessertpizza.html

About the Author

Dana Meachen Rau is an author, editor, and illustrator. A graduate of Trinity College in Hartford, Connecticut, she has written more than two hundred books for children, including nonfiction, biographies, early readers, and historical fiction. She likes to eat pizza with her family in Burlington, Connecticut.

About the Reading Consultant

Nanci R. Vargus, Ed.D., used to teach first grade. Now she works at the University of Indianapolis. Nanci helps young people become teachers. She supplies the pizza for her annual family reunion in California.

Marshall Cavendish Benchmark
99 White Plains Road
Tarrytown, NY 10591-5502
www.marshallcavendish.us

Copyright © 2009 by Marshall Cavendish Corporation
First Marshall Cavendish paperback edition, 2009

All Internet sites were correct at the time or printing.

Library of Congress Cataloging-in-Publication Data
Rau, Dana Meachen, 1971–
Pizza / by Dana Meachen Rau.
      p. cm. — (Benchmark Rebus : What's Cooking?)
Summary: "Easy to read text with rebuses explores different varieties of pizza"—Provided by publisher.
Includes bibliographical references.
ISBN 978-0-7614-2891-6 (HB)   ISBN 978-0-7614-3522-8 (PB)
1. Pizza--Juvenile literature. I. Title.
TX770.P58R39 2008
641.8'248—dc22
        2007021514

Editor: Christine Florie
Publisher: Michelle Bisson
Art Director: Anahid Hamparian
Series Designer: Virginia Pope

Photo research by Connie Gardner

Rebus images provided courtesy of *Dorling Kindersley.*

Cover photo by *age fotostock/SuperStock*

The photographs in this book are used with permission and through the courtesy of:
PhotoEdit: pp. 5, 13, 15 David Young Wolff; *The Image Works*: p. 7 Francis Dean/Dean Pictures; *Corbis*: p. 9 Nancy Ney; p. 11 J. Hall photocuisine; p. 19 Phil C. Chauncey; *Alamy*: p. 17 food folio; *Jupiter Images*: p. 21 Burke/Triolo Productions.

Printed in Malaysia
1 3 5 6 4 2